Getting married in church – again

David E. Flavell

Kevin Mayhew

First published in 2001 by
KEVIN MAYHEW LTD
Buxhall
Stowmarket
Suffolk IP14 3BW

0 1 2 3 4 5 6 7 8 9

ISBN 1 84003 684 2
Catalogue No 1500406

Cover design by Jonathan Stroulger
Edited and typeset by Elisabeth Bates
Printed and bound in Great Britain

Preface

This book is designed for those who have been divorced and want to get married again in church.

They might have several concerns:

- How will we be received by the minister?
- What are the practical details?
- Who does the paperwork?
- Can we be sure this marriage will work out?
- What do we do next?

All these questions and more are answered in this helpful little book. It is up to date with all the latest regulations and takes a contemporary look at getting married in church – again.

I hope you enjoy it.

Rev David E. Flavell
Liverpool, October 2000
http://www.evoevo.pwp.blueyonder.co.uk

Also by David E. Flavell, published by Kevin Mayhew:
Cooking Up Worship ISBN 1-84003-375-4

For Faith and Owen

Acknowledgements

I would like to thank the following people for helping with the manuscript: Bob Hills, Peter Grimwood, Martha Flavell, Ross and Memory Tracy, Neville and Pam Flavell, Fiona Hewitt, Marie Dove, David MacDonald, Rob Eastaway and Elaine Standish.

The cartoons are drawn by Dik LaPine.

The statistics come courtesy of either the Office for National Statistics, or from Dr Peter Brierley, Christian Research, as given in *Religious Trends* No 2, 2000/2001, published by HarperCollins and Christian Research, 1999.

Getting remarried in church

That's a stand-in minister – they wanted the bloke from 'Ballykissangel'.

So, you're thinking of getting remarried in church. But have you thought why?

Here are some possible reasons:

- Your family expects it.
- A church holds more guests than the Register Office.
- The Church stands for the importance of marriage – and so do you.
- You were brought up in a church.
- You want a nice white wedding.
- Going to church is a way of showing that this is a special occasion.
- It's not a 'proper' wedding in the Register Office.
- You want a new start and God's blessing.

Perhaps you haven't really thought about it. Perhaps you should!

After all, getting married in church is very different from getting married in a Register Office. The Church is more than a hotel with a cross on the wall. In church, we don't just make promises in front of each other, we make them before God.

Why does the Church make it so difficult to get married again if you have been divorced?

The Church doesn't set out to make it difficult. The Church is not deliberately trying to give you a hard time. The Church is not trying to make you or your partner feel guilty. After all, Christianity is about forgiveness.

The reason why the Church acts like this is because of the Bible. Christians use the Bible as their manual for living, and pay particular attention to the words of Jesus. If you don't have a Bible, then preparing for a marriage might be a good time to go and buy one. Most bookshops should be able to help. Ask for a modern, understandable version, like the Good News Bible, or the New International Version. You shouldn't have to pay a great deal.

Divorce

What does it mean to be divorced? It means more than just being separated, or having fallen out of love. In the same way that falling *in* love with somebody conveys no legal rights until there is a wedding, so leaving a partner escapes no legal obligations until there is a divorce.

Marriage is a legally binding contract which affects, amongst other things, inheritance. You can be separated from your wife, you can be at daggers drawn, you can be going through divorce proceedings, but if she dies without having made a will, you inherit everything she has. The legal obligation only ends when the divorce is finalised. In England and Wales, the first part of a divorce is the 'Decree Nisi', which is the preliminary stage. Then comes the 'Decree Absolute' which means that the marriage is legally over. *Without your Decree Absolute, you are still married.*

When you see your minister, you will need to bring a copy of your Decree(s) Absolute with you.

Later on, you will need to go to the Register Office to get your certificates to enable you to be married. Once again, you will need your Decree(s) Absolute to prove your eligibility to wed.

Things the Bible says about divorce

In the Gospel of Mark (10:2-12), Jesus talks about marriage and divorce. His enemies asked the seemingly straightforward question: 'Is it lawful for a man to divorce his wife? Yes or No?'

Now you might think that Jesus would want to give a straightforward answer to a straightforward question, but they were asking him to try to trap him. They knew what the Law said, but they also knew what the consequences were, and they wanted to put Jesus in a no-win situation.

Divorce was primarily an economic issue in the time of Jesus. A divorced woman was removed from her husband's household and could not return to her father's household. Nor could she seek another husband as she had no dowry, or money to bring with her into the marriage. A divorced woman had nowhere to go, no resources, and no alternative lifestyle available other than prostitution. If her husband divorced her, she would be destitute.

Under the Law of Moses, from the Old Testament, the Jews of the time *were* allowed to get divorced. This came from the book of Deuteronomy (24:1).

So the trap was, if Jesus said, 'Yes, you can divorce', the Pharisees would say, 'He has no morals.'

If Jesus said, 'No, you cannot divorce', they would say, 'Who do you think you are, disagreeing with the Law?'

They thought that they had him in a cleft stick, but Jesus wasn't so easily trapped. The response that Jesus made was based on compassion, and hopefully the Church today exercises compassion in its treatment of divorce.

Jesus asked them what the Law commanded. They replied that the Law said that a man could divorce his wife and send her away from home, just by writing a certificate.

At this point, Jesus changed the rules. He told the Pharisees that the reason men were allowed to be divorced was only because they were so selfish and hard-hearted. Jesus was not prepared to let them get away with this, and said that if a couple were joined together before God, they should not be separated.

The disciples asked for further clarification, and Jesus explained. 'Anyone who divorces his wife and marries another woman commits adultery *against her*.'

This was a major step forward. By equating divorce with adultery, Jesus was saying that a man who got rid of his wife because he didn't like her any more, was just as guilty as a man who stayed married yet had an affair. 'Do not commit adultery' was one of the Ten Commandments. It was strictly forbidden because of the damage that it did to the people committing it, and to their relationships with others. Jesus was making it clear that divorce was not something trivial, and that the wife was the victim of it.

This episode within the teaching of Jesus about divorce can also be found in the Gospel of Matthew (19:3-12). Here there is an extra bit of text that is not reported in Mark. Jesus allowed a man to divorce his wife if she had been unfaithful.

Arranged divorce

The exemption in Matthew's Gospel led directly to the Divorce Law in England after the 1857 Divorce Act. Prior to this, it took an Act of Parliament for each divorce!

The 1857 Act, and subsequent amendments, allowed a divorce if one of the parties was prepared to admit adultery. This led to 'organised unfaithfulness', where a couple would make arrangements for a photographer to 'catch' the husband in bed with another woman in a hotel room (often in Brighton) so that infidelity could be proved. Then the divorce would be allowed.

Clearly this was silly, expensive and labelled one person as the 'guilty' adulterous party. It brought the law into disrepute because people were being encouraged to lie in court. Also, if one of the parties did not want to be divorced, then nothing could be done.

The law was changed in the 1960s to make divorce less difficult, and so that people could tell the truth, that their relationship had ended, with or without the interference of a third party. Today divorce can be allowed because of unreasonable behaviour, or separation.

In both Mark's Gospel and Matthew's Gospel, Jesus is preventing innocent women being left with nothing, just because their husbands were fed up with them.

Change in society

Since biblical times, the position of women in society has changed completely. Although divorce is a guaranteed way to reduce your income and make lawyers rich, it does not usually lead to destitution, prostitution or economic collapse.

Because society has changed, people in unhappy marriages are now more free to leave one another.

Divorce can still be about poverty, guilt, unhappiness and sorrow, *but it is not the end of the world*, as it was in times gone by.

The Church in the modern world has had to decide how to respond to this change. When nobody was getting divorced, nobody was getting remarried, so it was not really an issue. Today two-fifths of weddings in England involve at least one person who has been married before.

The Church has responded to the biblical account of the words of Jesus in two ways:

Response One
One response is to say that the words of Jesus still literally stand today. 'Divorce was wrong in biblical times and it is wrong today. Jesus clearly states that there should be no marriage of divorced people, so that is what our church policy will be.'

Churches that hold this position include the Church of England (but watch this space) and some more conservative denominations. If you are turned away because one of you has been married before, it's nothing personal, that's just the way the rules are – with no exceptions.

'Yes, but,' people say, 'that's not fair!'

However, the Church never said that life *was* fair, and the rules are clear and set down by Jesus himself. If you don't like the rules, then complain to Jesus, not the Church.

'Yes, but,' people say, 'it wasn't my fault that we got divorced in the first place.'

Of course it is impossible for the Church to work out whose *fault* it was. That is even if *fault* is the right approach. Sometimes marriages break up not because one person is guilty and the other person innocent but because they just can't get on with one another. And the Church has neither the resources, nor the expertise, nor even the desire, to sort through all the evidence and then apportion blame. To do that job properly we would need a court, private investigators, sworn statements from witnesses and a team of barristers. Instead ministers are left with the problem of being expected to take the word of the people who come to see them.

What really happened?

Within six months of each other, a former husband and wife both married new partners at my church. When I asked each of them to describe their previous relationship, they gave a very different story as to whose *fault* it was that it ended. Which one of them was right? Whose word should I have believed?

The Decree Absolute forms do not help. In 1996, 70 per cent of all divorces were granted to wives and 30 per cent to husbands.[1] Does this really reflect the *faults* in these marriages?

In Mark's Gospel, Jesus does not forbid remarriage just for those who were at fault, but for *all* those who got divorced. In Matthew's Gospel, the only exemption clause is against those who have been unfaithful. For everyone else there is no question of finding *fault*. Instead, with the exception of unfaithfulness, the divorced couple are enjoined to stay together, rather than to seek new partners.

The *ideal* in this case is that the estranged couple are aided to get back together again, so that the marriage which was broken can be

1. Office for National Statistics Population Trends 1995, Spring 1999 Update.

made whole. Many couples find this distressing, because they have tried over and over again, and feel that they have failed and want to move on. However, there *are* cases where people become Christians after having been divorced and then get back together again, being remarried in church.

Response Two
The second response that the wider Church has made to the words of Jesus is to see them as being a compassionate shift from the previous position. Jesus did the most caring thing for the circumstances of the day. The Church should try to work out the most caring thing for today.

People are living longer. Women are economically independent. There is no need to stay in an unhappy marriage just because society wants it that way. Life has changed from how it was in years gone by. With a different world comes a different way of doing things, and a different approach to divorce and remarriage.

The Church should recognise that the world has changed, and be prepared to marry those who have been divorced, to forgive the *faults* on both sides and to offer them the love and care to start again.

Which response?

The Church recognises the tension between the two responses, and each individual minister will have to make their own policy. There is a huge diversity of opinion and practice, as marriage is an issue which arouses heated controversy. Some ministers will never marry divorcees, some will marry divorcees in 'appropriate circumstances', others will marry those who were not married in church last time, others will want to do a service which is different from the service for a first marriage.

So which denomination will marry us?

Finding a minister who will marry you varies from place to place. Within each denomination there are ministers who will *sometimes* marry those who have been divorced, and those who will *never* do those weddings.

You will have to check out the local situation. *There is no automatic right to be married*, just because you live in the area, or even if you are a member of a church. But wherever you go, you should receive a warm and caring welcome, even if they have to give you a negative answer.

By and large, you are *less* likely to find a minister to marry you in the Church of England, or the Roman Catholic Church. You are *more* likely (but not certain) to find a minister to marry you in the Church of Scotland, the Methodist Church, or the United Reformed Church. If getting married in church is important to you, then you may have to try more than one.

Why are there all these different kinds of Churches?

Each time there has been a revival in the life of the church, it has led to a new denomination being formed. This historical process means that today, there is a great variety of churches. This diversity is a good thing, because it gives you the opportunity to choose the church that is appropriate for you.

Try going to different churches in your area until you find one that feels right for you.

Wedding Blessing

An alternative service to the full marriage ceremony is a *Wedding Blessing*, officially called a 'Service of Prayers and Dedication after a Civil Marriage'. Some ministers will offer this to those they are unable to marry because they have been divorced.

For a Wedding Blessing, the marriage takes place in the Register Office first and then the couple come to church for a service. The format of the service is similar to a wedding, but there is no signing of the registers and no vows are made.

You walk down the aisle into church together as husband and wife and at the point in the service where the vows would come, a question along these lines is asked instead:

'Adam, you have already taken Eve to be your lawful wedded wife. Since you wish to recognise before God your desire for Christian marriage, I ask you therefore, will you love her, honour and keep her, and forsaking all others be faithful to her, so long as you both shall live?'

To which the answer is:

'With God's help I will.'

Then Eve gets her turn, and makes her response. There are hymns and readings and a sermon, just as in the official Marriage Service. The congregation are asked to support the couple with their prayers in the same way. At the end of the service the couple leave without signing the registers.

If getting *officially married* in church is important to you, then you may have to go to another denomination in your area. If having a service in a *particular church* is important to you, then you may have to choose a Wedding Blessing.

Discuss the issues with your minister. If you do opt for a Wedding Blessing, you will still have to book both the Register Office and the church well in advance.

Sometimes it is appropriate to do a Wedding Blessing for practical reasons (see the box overleaf).

Japanese wedding

I had a Japanese Christian, living in England, and wanting to bring his fiancée over from Japan to get married in the church. She didn't speak any English, and neither of them signed in Western script. It would still have been possible for them to be married in the church, but it was a lot easier for them to be married in the Register Office in Japan, and then come to England for a wedding blessing.

Who do these ministers think they are to judge us?

The minister does not judge you. If the Church only married perfect couples there would be no marriages. And of course the ministers are not perfect either!

In the Roman Catholic Church, there has to be a Church Court to decide whether the previous marriage can be annulled. To annul a marriage means to decide that it was never a valid marriage in the first place. The whole process takes a long time and you will have to contact your priest for guidance.

For the Protestant denominations, it is left to the conscience of each local minister to guide them as to their actions. A similar situation can be found with Christenings. Some ministers will baptise babies, some ministers will only baptise adults. They do not *judge* the adults or the babies, but their strong beliefs about the Church guide their actions. Those who only baptise adults, often offer an alternative 'dedication' service. This allows people to meet in church and give thanks to God for the child, without the theological act of baptism.

Ministers are not *judging* you if they say that they do not marry people who have been divorced. Instead, they have strong beliefs about the Church that guide the way they act. It may *feel* as though you are being judged, because nobody likes being rejected, but this is not the case.

Why isn't there a nationally agreed policy?

Part of the reason is the kind of people that ministers are. To be a bank manager or a dentist you don't have to take a strong view on religion or politics. Ministers do have strong views, by the very nature of their role, and getting them all to agree on anything is a miracle. The issue of marriage is left to the conscience of the local minister, as it is thought that they are in the best position to know the local situation. Many local ministers do have strong views on marriage, and will set their policy accordingly.

There's not much point arguing with the minister on the doorstep about the rights and wrongs of his or her view. You may as well ask them to change their religion while you're at it!

When you do find a minister who is prepared to marry those who have been divorced, he or she will want to share an interview with you. Once again this is not about *judging*. Instead, they will be interested in what you have to say about previous relationships, from a pastoral angle. For instance, is the new relationship responsible for the ending of the previous one? Have issues surrounding the previous marriage been resolved, such as childcare and maintenance payments? Are people still bearing grudges and harbouring resentment against a former spouse? Do members of the former spouse's family attend this church and would it be more sensitive to have the wedding elsewhere?

The Church does not want to find fault or to examine whether you are truly sorry for the failure of a previous relationship. This is not an inquisition. We assume that people who have been divorced *do* wish that life had turned out differently and have not taken their vows lightly. There may be the occasional pop-star who cockily regards marriage as just a game, but most people who have been through a divorce see it as one of the worst periods of their lives. The Church is here to help in the healing, and also to help avoid the same mistakes being made twice.

One of the difficulties is that there is an increasing number of divorces from second and subsequent marriages. In 1997, 28 per cent of all divorces were second or subsequent divorces.[1] The Church has to take seriously the problem that a marriage involving at least one of the parties having been divorced before is *more* likely to end in separation than a first marriage. One study suggested that a man who had been divorced is 50 per cent more likely than a bachelor of the same age to divorce for a second time, and a woman who has been divorced is twice as likely to divorce for a second time.[2]

You would expect the minister to discuss very carefully with two 16-year-olds the meaning of marriage. In the same way, the Church would be shirking its responsibility to you if it failed to ask the difficult questions of those coming to be married again in church. It is not a wish to pry, or to find blame, but a desire to help clear the issues.

After all, how many divorced people will say, 'I should never have married that person', and wished that the minister had asked more searching questions the first time round? Those who have been divorced will know just how important it is to get things right this time, and how it can be far better never to have married at all, rather than to have married and then split.

Your minister is acting primarily as a *pastor* and not as a *judge*. It is his or her job to care for you as much as possible. Caring for somebody does not always mean saying 'yes' to everything they want. Sometimes the best friend is one who tells you the truth, but loves you just the same. Ideally your local minister will take this caring role seriously.

The Register Office will always be prepared to marry you as long as you pass their requirements: You are of age, you are not already married, and you are not too closely genetically related. Their weddings are legal ceremonies.

The Church will be happy to marry you as long as you pass its requirements: All the above, plus the ability to stand before God and make informed promises that you are going to keep. Church weddings are legal ceremonies, but also dedications before God.

1. Office for National Statistics Dataset PV97416.
2. Office for National Statistics Population Trends 32, Summer 1983, page 14. Also roughly confirmed in 1995.

But isn't it a minister's job to do weddings?

Funnily enough, it isn't. Ministers spend their time

- Preparing and leading Worship Services
- Encouraging and evangelising
- Public Speaking
- Running Bible Study and Prayer groups
- Visiting the sick and needy
- Visiting schools, hospitals and prisons
- Administering the Church
- Being part of the local community as School Governors, committee members, trustees, etc.

And also doing baptisms, weddings and funerals!

Many people will include weddings in a minister's job description, but nowhere in the Bible does it say, 'Go out and perform as many weddings as possible'. Instead most ministers see their role as leading worship, caring for the flock, and reaching out to those in need. It is as part of this wider vision that they do weddings.

If you are looking for someone whose only job is to do weddings and nothing else, then you will have to go to the Elvis Chapel in Las Vegas!

Making the same mistake – again

So why are people who have been divorced and remarried more likely to divorce again than those who have never been divorced?

Part of the reason is that once you have been through the stigma of divorce, you are not going to be so frightened of doing it again. Secondly, the kind of person who won't stand for unhappiness in one relationship is not likely to tolerate it in another.

However, the third reason is that sometimes people marry the same kind of person again. This is particularly true, for instance, of women in abusive relationships. Some women find themselves in a pattern of abuse. They are beaten by their husbands, and when they finally move on, they become involved with another partner or husband who also beats them. It is only when they are able to break the pattern that they can start to form healthy relationships.

But this isn't just true of abuse. Some men have a 'Knight in Shining Armour' complex. They are particularly attracted to needy women and think that they can solve their problems for them. When it turns out that they can't solve the problems, or when the woman gets on her feet and doesn't need them any more, they move on to the next relationship.

Or there can be other recurring themes in your relationships. Maybe you are a poor communicator, or an over-achiever, or you always have to be in charge? Or maybe you always go for submissive types?

Our conscious mind seeks out the kind of partner we *want*, but our unconscious mind is looking for the partner we *need*. If you find yourself being attracted to the wrong kind of person over and over again, ask yourself what need in you they might be meeting.

Look at what is different this time. Is your new partner very different from the old one? What attracted you to them? Was it the same things? How does your new partner resolve problems – creatively or otherwise? Are you older and wiser this time, or just older? Have you resolved all the issues from your previous relationship, or is further counselling needed for you, or for you and your new partner?

Your minister will help you look at all these issues. It's not enough to say, 'It's different this time because I love him.' Most people *do* really love the person they marry, especially on the day the wedding takes place. The problem is not the quality of the love on day one, but the difficulty of maintaining that love on day two and beyond.

It's important not to bring your first spouse into the new relationship. They have no business in what is going on now. This is not only about them not appearing at the door all the time, although for those with children from a previous relationship there is going to be at least some contact.

Instead, it means that you must not be constantly comparing your new partner with the past in a negative light. Your ex-wife may have had a high-paying job and then come home and waited on you hand and foot, but that has absolutely nothing to do with your new wife.

Your ex-husband may have told you that he was going fishing, when really he was seeing another woman. That doesn't mean that when your new husband takes up fishing, he is thinking of having an affair.

It is important to let your new relationship develop without a negative influence from the previous relationship. This negative influence can happen in all sorts of subtle and unconscious ways, where something will remind you of how you were made to feel in the past, and you will overreact.

This marriage is a brand-new relationship, a brand-new start. Let it be so.

The best ex in the world

The preacher stood up and asked the congregation – 'is there anybody here who can tell me there has ever been a perfect man?'
He paused for dramatic effect, when a hand went up at the back.
'There has been a perfect man?' he asked incredulously.
'Yes,' said the man with his hand up. 'My wife's late first husband.'

They didn't make this fuss last time I was married

If there was little preparation the last time you were married, maybe there should have been more. Marriage preparation can save a lot of heartache later. Many churches run courses, but if yours does not, there are marriage encounter groups you can join. These allow you to meet with other couples in similar situations and learn from, and with, one another. They are listed in the resources section of this book.

What kind of wedding do you want – this time?

Seven wedding myths

- You have to have bridesmaids
- You have to have a best man
- The father has to give away the bride
- The bride must wear white
- The bride must have a bouquet
- The bride must promise to obey
- You have to sing *All things bright and beautiful*

Some people want to do exactly the opposite of what they had before. If there were loads of bridesmaids, they want none. If it was in the morning, they want the afternoon. If there were traditional hymns, they now want modern.

Part of this idea is to 'fix' all that went wrong last time by being very different this time. However, there are few marriages which go wrong because of what happens at the wedding ceremony. Instead the perfect day can be followed by years of unhappiness, or a complete fiasco can be followed by a wonderful marriage. The success of the wedding is not a metaphor for what is to come, although you may find out a lot about your partner as you share in the organisation together!

Instead, the wedding should represent the personalities of both you and your partner. It is an opportunity for a new start, a moving on, a forgetting of the past and a brand-new way of doing things. You are forgiven and free. This is not the time for settling old scores and getting your own back:

'I always wanted bridesmaids in blue, but I had to settle for lilac last time. There's no way I'm making the same mistake twice.'

When should we get married?

The rules state that the marriage must be 'solemnised' between the hours of 8am and 6pm. However, if you get married very early in the day, it may be inconvenient for anybody coming from a distance. If you get married late in the day, it leaves you very late for a reception and then a journey if you are going on honeymoon. So most weddings take place between 10am and 2pm.

The vast majority still occur on a Saturday. If you are booking two years in advance, or in the winter, you should find that the church and the reception venue are available. But if the church is very popular, or you leave things very late, you could have problems.

One alternative is to get married on a Friday. This has the advantage that it should be easier (and can be cheaper) to book a reception. Also, it gives your guests from out of town a more memorable wedding to attend. Instead of spending all day Saturday getting to the wedding, enjoying the party, sleeping it off, and then lurching home on Sunday, they can come to the wedding on Friday, then have all day Saturday to look around the area, and then go home at their own pace on Sunday. Finally your minister will thank you that they can do their work on a work day, rather than on a Saturday when they could be at home with their family.

Cup Final day

Each year, on the second or third Saturday in May, the FA Cup Final is held. This is a very bad day to have your wedding for at least four reasons:

- Half your guests will try to spend all their time in the bar, watching the match on TV
- The other guests won't be able to get to the bar for the crowd watching the TV
- The minister will be in a hurry to get home to watch
- Everyone will remember your wedding for the score in the game

Money

The average cost of a wedding today is more than £10,000. However, there is no need to spend more than £60. The certificates from the Register Office will set you back about £30 each. The cost of the church varies, but if you are a member at a church, the minister will often do the service for free. Then all you need are two other adult witnesses to the ceremony. *All other spending is optional.*

When people say that they can't afford to get married, what they are really saying is that they can't afford to get married *in the style they would like.*

Being well experienced at weddings, I have seen one couple spend money on having fifteen bridesmaids, another having a horse and carriage and yet another on a marquee for two hundred people. They didn't need to do that, but they chose to do it. Just because that was their choice does not mean that it has to be your choice.

Marriage certificates are not licences to spend money – it just feels that way.

Certificates

In the old days you could get married at short notice by Special Licence. This was very romantic, but has been discontinued. As of 1 January 2001 you must apply for two certificates, which must be identical in every respect, one for the bride and one for the groom.

These certificates can be obtained from the Register Office **up to twelve months** before the wedding. The minimum notice you can give is **fifteen days** before the wedding is to take place. Both bride and groom need to attend in person, preferably together. You cannot send somebody else to act as your representative. You will need to take the following information:

- Place, date and time of the wedding.
- The Decree Absolute for those who have been married before.
- Full names (including the embarrassing middle names) and occupations of bride, groom, bride's father and groom's father.

- Ages of bride and groom. Both must be over 16 and parental consent is needed in England and Wales for those aged 16 and 17 (but not in Scotland, which is why couples used to elope to Gretna Green. The age for parental consent in England used to be 21).
- Full address(es) for bride and groom. Both bride and groom must have been resident in their given address(es) for at least **seven days**.
- Any former names for bride and groom.
- Nationality of bride and groom.
- Proof of identity. This usually means a passport, although if this is not available, two documents, such as a cheque book, cheque guarantee card, store/credit card or a birth certificate issued at or near the time of the registration of your birth would generally be acceptable. Photocopies are unlikely to be accepted.

The Register Office only covers the local 'Registration District'. This is usually the same as the local council area. This means that if you pay rates or rents to Liverpool City Council, you need to go to the Liverpool Register Office. If both of you live in Liverpool, then both of you have to go in person and pick up your two certificates.

If one of you lives in Liverpool, and the other lives just over the border in Knowsley, *then you each have to go to your own Register Office* and register separately. Remember, the certificates must be identical. Make sure you have the correct details!

If you both live in Knowsley, but the church you want to get married in is in Liverpool, then you either have to state that the church is your usual place of worship, *or* that there is no church of that particular denomination in your local area. In either case, your Superintendent Registrar at the Register Office will be able to advise you.

Some churches are not registered for marriages. In these cases, one of the registrars from the local office will have to give permission (this does not happen automatically) and then attend in person to witness the marriage. Book early to avoid disappointment and remember that this will incur an additional fee.

If one of you lives in Scotland, then the law is slightly different. You have to get a 'Certificate of no impediment to marriage' from your Scottish District Registrar.

If one of you lives in Northern Ireland, you will need a certificate from the Registrar of your District in Northern Ireland. You cannot use a certificate from the Republic of Ireland to prove eligibility for marriage, as legally it counts as a separate country.

If you want to get married in Scotland or Northern Ireland, the law is different again. See the resources section at the end of this book.

If one of you is serving at sea in the Royal Navy, then the Ship's Captain acts as the Registrar, and issues the certificate.

Once you have 'given notice' to the Registrar(s) of your forthcoming wedding, your details will be displayed at the Register Office for fifteen days, so that any interested party can make an objection. (They can only make an objection on legal grounds, not because they think the wedding is a great mistake!)

After fifteen days or more have passed, you must collect the certificates in person and give them to the minister. This is a legal requirement. The undisputed rule is 'No Certificates – no Wedding'. The only exception to this rule is the Banns in the Church of England (see box).

Never mind the Banns, here's the Certificate

The Banns are only read if you are getting married in the Church of England.

The Banns come from the days when most people couldn't read and theoretically all of us lived in a village and everybody belonged to the Church of England. So when an announcement was made in Church that Adam Edenson (farmer) and Eve Snakesmith (dairymaid) were getting married next month, the whole population of the village would have been there, and any objections could have been registered.

At least that was the theory. Of course, even then some people lived in larger towns, and there never has been a time when the Anglicans were the only church in England.

When other church denominations were allowed to perform weddings, they used the certificate system. Register Office weddings were first permitted in 1836.

If the person you are going to marry is a foreign national, then there are more complications, especially if they have been divorced. They will need to have been in the United Kingdom at least **twenty-two days** before the wedding, **seven days** to prove UK residency and then **fifteen days** to get the certificates. If they still live abroad, then consult the British Embassy in their country as soon as possible, otherwise see your Superintendent Registrar. The process can take a long time.

Marriage Certificates

After the wedding, your minister will send back your Certificates of Eligibility to the Register Office, along with a copy of the record of your wedding. This completes the legal paperwork.

The minister will issue a copy wedding certificate. This document will be requested in due course by your Bank, Passport Office and all the other bureaucrats you can think of.

The details included are name, age, condition (see box), occupation, (natural) fathers' names and occupations, place and date of wedding, your signatures, the minister's signature, and the signatures of at least two reliable witnesses.

Condition

'Condition' just means your marital status before this wedding.

- Bachelor for a man who hasn't been married before
- Spinster for a woman who hasn't been married before
- Widow for a woman whose husband has died
- Widower for a man whose wife has died
- Previous Marriage Dissolved for each person who has been divorced, or where the previous spouse is missing, presumed dead
- Previous Marriage Annulled where the Court has made an annullment

---

Hymns

The chances are that your local church will have more than a thousand hymns to choose from. Some of these may be familiar, others you may not know. It is worth doing a little bit of research to find something you would like, rather than just 'the usuals'. If you want something out of the ordinary, then it is only fair to give the church plenty of notice.

Classic wedding hymns

All things bright and beautiful
At the name of Jesus
Amazing grace
Be thou my vision
Because he lives
Bind us together
Give me oil in my lamp
Great is thy faithfulness
Guide me, O thou great Jehovah
He's got the whole world in his hands
How great thou art
Lead us, Heavenly Father, lead us
Lord of all hopefulness, Lord of all joy
Love divine, all loves excelling
Make me a channel of your peace
Morning has broken
O Jesus, I have promised
O perfect love
One more step along the world I go
Praise, my soul, the King of heaven
The King of love my shepherd is
What a friend we have in Jesus
Will your anchor hold in the storms of life?

Not to mention 'Rescue the perishing' or 'Fight the good fight'!

Other music

Traditionally, the entrance is to 'Here comes the bride' and the exit to the 'Wedding March'. Other choices are Bach's 'Toccata', 'Crown Imperial' or 'Trumpet Voluntary'. Again, if you expect the church to provide the musical accompaniment, you need to give plenty of notice, in case the organist finds it difficult.

Modern music can be problematic. There is the urban myth about the substitute organist, who was told that the bride wanted the theme from *Robin Hood* as she came down the aisle. She was expecting Bryan Adams' 'Everything I do, I do it for you', but she got the 1950s TV series 'Robin Hood, Robin Hood, riding through the glen.'

You should check the words to see what the song is really about. A favourite love song is Whitney Houston's 'I will always love you'. That's a song expressing sadness at a love affair that cannot be, and saying that even though we have to part, our love will always be there. That song might be appropriate in other circumstances, but not for a wedding. If you must score an own-goal, then choose Gladys Knight & the Pips' classic 'It should have been me', because that's a better song anyway.

If you are going to have a tape, rather than use the church musicians, make sure that it is powerful enough and that it is going to be operated by somebody who knows what they are doing. The 'Coronation March' may sound wonderful played by the Band of the Royal Marines, but it may not sound so good on a tape recorder that distorts.

What about walking down the aisle?

How do I know which side to go on? And who should do it? And can I have more than one best man? And what colour should the page-boys wear?

The answer to these and countless other questions can be found in a book on wedding etiquette. However, you don't have to do what the book says. There are no hard and fast rules, just a great number of traditions. These vary in different parts of the country. Some of them are designed to bring good luck, but that doesn't mean that if you fail to do them, then your marriage will fail.

In the north-east it is considered lucky and a sign of good fortune for the groom to throw coins to the local children as the couple come out of the church. In Yorkshire it is thought lucky for a sweep to attend the wedding.

The Church is concerned that you have a good, healthy relationship with each other, and that you start off down the path of Christian Marriage. The Church is not concerned that you follow local superstitions, because they are not going to make the difference between your marriage succeeding or failing.

In all these things, your minister will advise. He or she will help you think through all the different ideas you have, so that you can have a wedding that is appropriate for you. The minister will guide and direct you, and almost certainly run a rehearsal so that there will be no unfortunate surprises on the day.

Once again you don't need to have any of the ceremonial. The bride does not have to wear white. You can both walk to the church. There only have to be two other adult witnesses. There doesn't have to be confetti (in fact churches often ban confetti because of the amount of work involved in cleaning it up). The important thing is that this is a Christian Marriage before God. If you just want the ceremonial, then there are stately homes and large hotels which will be happy to cater for you – at a price.

Should I employ an amateur photographer? My Uncle Eric takes snaps.

The usual rule-of-thumb with photographers is to compare them with hairdressers. If you are going to use a mirror, and cut your own hair for the ceremony, then Uncle Eric will do fine. Otherwise, use professionals for both jobs.

The churches still do more first weddings as compared to Register Offices, but coming up fast on the rails are these other venues such as football grounds or hotels (more than 10 per cent of all weddings in 1998).[1] Second weddings are 18 per cent at the church, and 82 per cent at the Register Office or other venues. In 1998 41.4 per cent of all weddings (religious and secular) involved at least one person who had been married before.[2]

We're already living together. Does this matter?

Whoever's house you live in, the Church will give you a warm welcome. In 1994, 60 per cent of all marriages in England and Wales involved couples who lived together (cohabited) first, and 41 per cent of all Church Marriages.[3] So the Church is used to it and it won't be a great surprise.

But getting married is very different from cohabiting. Being married is not just living together with a certificate.

Cohabiting is like moving to another country. You go to live in the country of 'Matrimony', but retain your old passport from the country of 'Singleness'. You keep your old nationality and allegiance and can always go back. As long as times are good, you stay. In due course, if it works out, you become a naturalised citizen of the new state and get a 'passport' in the form of a wedding certificate.

It sounds like an attractive and sensible way of proceeding, but actually it makes you up to 80 per cent more likely to get divorced subsequently.[4]

It turns out that it is a lot better for a couple to move to 'Matrimony' and pledge allegiance to the new state all in one go. You give up all

1. Office for National Statistics Population Trends 99, Spring 2000 report: Marriages in England and Wales during 1998, Table 1.
2. Ibid.
3. UK Christian Handbook, Religious Handbook No 2, 2000/2001, Table 4.6.3.
4. Pre-marital cohabitation and the probability of subsequent divorce: analyses using new data from the General Household Survey. John Haskey Population Statistics Division, OPCS in Population Trends No 68, Summer 1992.

thought of 'Singleness', where you have come from, and put your energy to the new country. You take on your new documentation, and dispose of your old allegiances. You are going to stay in 'Matrimony' come what may, whether times are good or bad. You will only move back to 'Singleness' in the most disastrous of circumstances. Your commitment is to 'Matrimony', however it is governed, and not to the pursuit of happiness.

Only 5 per cent of those who married in 1995 after previously cohabiting said that the main reason was the influence of parents or friends (although nearly twice as many women as men said this). So the vast majority of couples were making their own decision.

Instead, 34 per cent said that they wanted to make the relationship stronger and more secure, and a further 8 per cent said that they felt that the 'trial marriage' had worked (although nearly twice as many men as women took this approach). 21 per cent of previously cohabiting couples said that their main reason for getting married involved the arrival of children.

There were many other thoughts offered, but one anecdotal reason why people who live together get married is that they don't know what to do next. They can stay as they are, which may make one partner uncomfortable, especially if that person wants children. They can split up, which makes both partners uncomfortable because they do love each other. Or they can get married and see what happens next.

This can lead to a very common but unfortunate situation, where a couple have lived together for several years, then get married, and split up within a short time. Be sure you are getting married because you really want to, and not because you don't know what to do next.

Loneliness and having no partner is a state that many people want to avoid. Yet it is not your partner's job to make you happy. You can be lonely even within a marriage, and that is a far worse place to be. The next section explains more.

Our minister – she looks awfully young

It's bad enough when the policemen look younger, but if you think that your minister looks like a teenager, you really are getting on a bit. Rest assured that your minister will have been fully trained in leading weddings. More experienced hands can easily have performed hundreds of weddings. So they know what they are doing. Your minister will guide you through the entire service.

If you would prefer a man rather than a woman (or a woman rather than a man) to perform the wedding, then unfortunately this is not possible. Each minister has a particular church (or churches) for which they are responsible and it would be entirely inappropriate and unprofessional to take a wedding in somebody else's church, just because the couple did not like the local minister. The ministry of women is just as valid as the ministry of men, so please do not put anybody in a difficult position by asking.

It is possible to request for a relative or family friend who is a minister to share in the ceremony, but this is entirely at the discretion of the local minister, and they will still have to preside officially.

What is Christian marriage?

Why is it different? What is it about?

Many people expect the Church to be in favour of 'family values' and to say that the marriage relationship is the most important relationship there is. *But the Church doesn't say that.*

Instead, the most important relationship for Christians is the relationship between us and God. This is even more important than the relationships between husband and wife, mother and daughter, father and son. That's quite a claim and it has enormous implications for the way we live our lives.

The relationship between husband and wife is meant to mirror the relationship between God and us. That relationship is permanent, always loving and forgiving.

However, we know that marriages made on earth do fail. We know that they are not always permanent. When people get divorced, there is pain and sadness in the broken relationship. This is the same pain that God feels about each one of us, when we are separated from him.

God wants us to love him. And he is always ready to take us back, even when we have abandoned him and rejected him and looked elsewhere for love. That is God's nature – always wanting us back. God doesn't want us to impress him – we can't. God wants us to love him.

In Christian marriage, we recognise that the love that God has for us is even stronger than the love that a husband or wife can have for one another. After all, God loves more than any human ever can.

In Christian marriage, our *first* relationship is with God, and our *second* relationship is with our husband or wife.

This seems bizarre to start with. Here we are, getting married, pledging allegiance to each other only, for all eternity, and now the Church wants us to put God into the equation. Surely marriage is for two, not three?

But it does make sense. Marriage is for three. Not bride, groom and mother-in-law, but bride, groom and God.

A famous Christian called Oswald Chambers put it like this:

> Most of the suffering in human life comes because we refuse to be disillusioned. For instance, if I love a human being, and do not love God, I demand of that man or woman an infinite satisfaction which they can't give. I demand of them every perfection and every rectitude, and when I do not get it, I become cruel and vindictive and jealous.

Husbands and wives are not perfect. They cannot be all that we want them to be, because they are only human.

Many people go through life thinking that if only they can get married, then they will be happy. But it doesn't work like that. You can't expect your husband or wife to make you happy. That's not their job. They are there to support and comfort you, to help and be a companion, but that doesn't mean that they are going to make you happy, just because you marry them.

It's a bit like money. Money can't buy you happiness, although it sure takes the sting out of being poor. Marriage can't make you happy, although it sure takes the sting out of being alone. The problem is that you can have poverty of life with plenty of money, and you can have loneliness within a relationship.

What happens is that after a while, the discovery is made that the husband or wife has not made you happy. Instead, you have the same outlook as you did before you got married. This leads people to the mistaken conclusion that they must have married the wrong person, so off they go, looking for the person 'out there' who *is* going to make them happy. They go through relationship after relationship, looking for 'the one'.

In the same way, don't think that you have the power to make your husband or wife happy. If they have issues in their lives that need dealing with, it's unlikely that you on your own will have all the answers.

What people are searching for in all this is God. God is at the heart of all our searching for meaning in life, for purpose and for contentment. When we find God, then we find what we are looking for.

That doesn't mean to say that Christians are always happy and that bad things will never happen to them. What it does mean is that Christians look to God to provide their meaning in life, and they look to love their husband and wife under God's love. This is a lot healthier than looking to a husband or wife to provide the ultimate meaning in life, because that is asking too much of a human being.

Once we don't expect a husband or a wife to make us happy, we can get on with appreciating them for who they are, and for all the great things about them. We can enjoy being married for the fact that we like our partners, and that they are good to be with, rather than having the pressure of expecting them to be perfect.

Do Christian marriages never fail, then?

Unfortunately they do sometimes fail. There are no guarantees that the relationship between husband and wife will always work out. Christian marriage is not an insurance policy.

In fact, becoming a Christian is not an insurance policy. If anything, becoming a Christian is more likely to lead to greater demands, because caring for others is not always easy or comfortable.

However, there are guarantees that God's love will never run out. If our ultimate meaning comes from God, then we will never be let down. A husband or wife is only human and cannot meet our very deepest needs. God can.

The point is that being married in church does not necessarily lead to a Christian marriage. If you want this kind of relationship with each other, then ask your minister what it means to be a Christian, or see the section of this book (near the end) entitled 'Who is Jesus?'

Here come the happy couple! Get ready with the pea-shooters!

What happens next?

The next thing to do is to go and see your minister. He or she will want to talk things over with you and discuss all the issues. A good way to get a feel for the church and its ethos, is to attend the service on a Sunday. Hopefully the minister will be there (some have more than one church) when you are, and will be able to arrange an appointment for you to meet.

When you go for your interview, don't forget that you will need to have your paperwork with you, particularly your Decree Absolute.

Once you have booked the church, *then* you can go ahead and make reservations for all the other things you might want, such as the reception, the car, the photographer, the video and everything else. Remember that these are all optional – not compulsory. Don't forget to spend your money on the right things – it will go very quickly.

In the meantime, why not try the 'Who wants to be happily married?' quiz at the end of this booklet?

Whatever happens next, may the Lord bless you and keep you for evermore.

Amen.

Things they say about marriage

Incompatibility is at the heart of a marriage as long as one's got the income and the other's got the pattability.
Amanda Stone

A Hollywood wedding is one where they take each other for better or for worse – but not for long.
E. C. McKenzie

The highest happiness on earth is in marriage. Every person who is happily married is a successful person, even when they have failed in everything else.
William Lyon Phelps

Marriage is an edifice that must be rebuilt every day.
André Maurois

Marry in haste and repent at leisure.
Anon

It is a truth universally acknowledged that a single man in possession of a good fortune must be in want of a wife.
Jane Austen

An archaeologist is the best husband any woman can have: the older she gets, the more interested he is in her.
Agatha Christie

[Second marriage is] the triumph of hope over experience.
Samuel Johnson

By all means marry. If you get a good wife you will become very happy; if you get a bad one, you will become a philosopher – and that is also good.
Socrates, the Greek Philosopher

Who is Jesus?

Jesus was born about 2,000 years ago into an ordinary family. No one knows the exact date of his birth, or the exact place of his birth, except that it was somewhere in Bethlehem, a small town even today.

Jesus lived, taught and died in the country of Israel. He taught ordinary people about the coming of the kingdom of God, not an earthly kingdom, but a kingdom of peace, that people could find in their own lives. He healed the sick, forgave those who needed to be forgiven, and lived with the outcasts of society. Those who were rich and powerful did not like this, because he spoke with authority, and made their religious leaders look foolish.

They decided to have him killed, and rushed him through a kangaroo court so that nobody could stop them. The best moral system and legal system that humanity had yet produced was responsible for his death. They nailed him to a tree to warn others not to mock the authorities. Nobody knows exactly where he was crucified, but it was somewhere just outside the old city of Jerusalem.

The difference between Jesus and any other man is that God raised Jesus from the dead. Even though the world thought they had got rid of him, they hadn't. No individual has changed history more than Jesus, the Son of God. There are now more Christians in the world than ever before.

Christians believe that the death and resurrection of Jesus is of vital importance. Now Jesus has risen from the dead, and conquered death, we too can live for ever. We can be forgiven the times we have fallen short of God's standards. God is perfect, so we all fall short of his standards many times in our lives. We need forgiveness. How can we be forgiven? What do we have to do to be reconciled with God? Jesus said that he came into our world not to be our judge but to be our Saviour. He came not to condemn us for our failings but to help us overcome them. Christians believe that *whatever* we have done, *whoever* we are, *wherever* we have been, we can be forgiven. It doesn't cost money, it doesn't need good works, all we have to do is put our trust in Jesus, and believe in him.

If Christianity is true, it is of world-shattering importance. If it is false it is of no importance at all. What Christianity can never be is moderately important. Many people think of themselves as Christians, but it is worth asking what their idea of a 'Good Christian' amounts to. Often it turns out to mean nothing more than vaguely believing that there is a God, or subscribing to broadly civilised standards of behaviour. These are weak substitutes for the real thing, and those who set their sights as low as this, will have little difficulty in being 'Christians'.

One of the key hallmarks of a true Christian is a sense of gratitude to God, a thankfulness for his love and forgiveness. Baptism as a child makes no difference – if you are old enough to get married, you are old enough to make a decision for yourself. Having parents who go to church makes no difference – Christianity is not hereditary. Being born into a Christian family does not make you a Christian, just as being born in a stable doesn't make you a horse! Real Christianity is life-changing.

We all still fail and few Christians are perfect, but if you want to *try* and follow Jesus, then that is enough. God accepts all those who sincerely turn to him, whatever they have done in the past. Becoming a Christian is as much a new start to life as getting married! If you would like to know more about what it *really* means to be a Christian, then come along any time to the church.

Or contact (no stamp required):
Christian Enquiry Agency
Freepost
London
SE1 7YX

http://www.christianity.org.uk

Who wants to be happily married?

1. How old are you?

Under 20	Under 25	Under 30
Under 40	Under 50	50 or over

2. How old is your partner?

Under 20	Under 25	Under 30
Under 40	Under 50	50 or over

3. What is the age difference between you?

less than 2 years	less than 5 years	less than 10 years
less than 15 years	less than 20 years	20 years or more

4. How long have you known each other?

less than 6 months	less than 1 year	less than 2 years
more than 2 years		

5. Have you been divorced?

Neither of you	One of you	Both of you

6. Are you living together?

Yes	No

7. Is one of you pregnant?

Yes	No

8. Do either of you have children?

No	One of you	Both of you

9. Did either of you get married in church last time?

Yes	No

10. Are you regular churchgoers?

No   One of you   Both of you

11. Do you belong to different religions?

Yes   No

12. Do you have divorced brothers or sisters?

Yes   No

13. Are your parents still married?

Happily Married   Unhappily Married
Divorced/Separated   Widowed

14. Are your partner's parents still married?

Happily Married   Unhappily Married
Divorced/Separated   Widowed

15. Do your parents approve?

Yes   Yes and No   No, neither set approves

16. Do your friends approve?

Yes   Sort of   No

17. Are you both in work?

Yes   No

18. Do you agree about money?

Yes   No

19. Have you ever split up with each other?

Never   Once   Twice
Three times   More than three times

20. Do you love each other?

Yes   More than anybody ever before

Answers

1. Score 1 for under 20, 2 for under 25, 4 for under 30, 6 for under 40, 8 for under 50 and 10 for 50 or over. Teenage brides comprise 3.5 per cent of all weddings, but more than 20 per cent of subsequent divorces. Boys take a little more time to grow up – males under 25 at marriage make up 17 per cent of all weddings but 48 per cent of all divorces.[1]

2. Again, score 1 for under 20, 2 for under 25, 4 for under 30, 6 for under 40, 8 for under 50 and 10 for 50 or over.

3. Score 8 for under 2, 7 for under 5, 6 for under 10, 4 for under 15, 2 for under 20 and 1 for 20 and over.

4. Score 1 for less than 6 months, 2 for less than a year, 6 for less than 2 years and 10 for more than 2 years. Divorce is 6 times as likely for the under-6-month group and twice as likely for the under-one-year group.[2]

5. Score 6 for neither of you, 4 for one of you, 2 for both of you. Score 1 if either of you has been divorced twice.

6. Score 1 for yes, 5 for no. Those marrying in the early '80s after cohabiting were 50 per cent more likely to be divorced after 5 years and 60 per cent more likely after 8 years. Women born in the '60s and under 20 at age of marriage were twice as likely to divorce if they had cohabited.[3]

1. Office for National Statistics Datasets PV9542B and PM95313A.
2. *Who Divorces?* Barbara Thornes & Jean Collard 1979. Routledge. ISBN 07100 01878
3. Pre-marital cohabitation and the probability of subsequent divorce: analyses using new data from the General Household Survey. John Haskey Population Statistics Division, OPCS In Population Trends No 68, Summer 1992.

7. Score 1 for yes and 15 for no. Those who are pregnant when they get married are half as likely again to get divorced as those who are not. This is even more pronounced with teenagers.[1] Subtract another 5 points if the bride is under twenty years old.

8. Score 1 for any answer. There is no evidence yet that the number of children involved has an effect. Those couples who have children together are *less* likely to get divorced, maybe because they 'stick together for the sake of the children', or maybe because 'childlessness' can sometimes be a source of conflict and unhappiness.

9. Score 1 for either answer. Location of wedding has no significant effect on the likelihood of subsequent divorce.

10. Score 1 for no, 2 for one of you, 3 for both of you. There are slightly fewer divorces amongst churchgoers, particularly those who say grace before meals. (This is probably an indication of a higher level of commitment to Christianity, rather than that saying grace prevents divorce.)

11. Score 4 for no, score 1 for yes. Belonging to different religions can cause tensions between other members of the family. Also your basic values and the assumptions you make about marriage can be different.

12. Score 3 for no, 1 for yes. Those who have siblings who have divorced are slightly more likely to divorce. This may be because the stigma has been removed, or there may be other factors predisposing towards divorce that have already been made evident in the siblings.[2]

13. Score 5 for happy, 1 for unhappy, 1 for separated or divorced, 5 for widowed. Those who perceive that their parents are unhappily married are as likely to separate as those whose parents are divorced.[3]

1. *Who Divorces?* Barbara Thornes & Jean Collard 1979. Routledge. ISBN 07100 01878   2. Ibid.   3. Ibid.

14. Score 5 for happy, 1 for unhappy, 1 for separated or divorced, 5 for widowed. Those who get divorced are significantly more likely to perceive that their partner's parents have an unhappy marriage.[1]

15. Score 30 for yes, 10 for yes and no, 1 for neither. Premarital parental approval comes in a positive ratio of five to one for continuing marriages, but only fifty-fifty for those who subsequently divorce. Listen to your folks – they could be right.[2]

16. Score 5 for yes, 3 for sort of, 1 for no. Friends don't know you nearly as well as your parents.

17. Score 2 for yes, score 1 for no. Despite romantic idealism, marriage can be harmed by practical issues such as unemployment and shortage of cash. Money can't buy you love, but it sure takes the sting out of poverty.

18. Score 2 for yes, score 1 for no, but don't be fooled. An American study showed that 90 per cent of couples getting married thought that money would not be an issue for them, but 80 per cent of people getting divorced said that money had been a real bone of contention. Clearly some people have an unrealistic expectation of married life when it comes to money.

19. Score 10 for never, 10 for once, 4 for twice, 2 for three times and 1 for more than that. Splitting up once before doesn't make any difference to your divorce prospects. The fact that you have come back together shows that you are capable of making up. However, the more times you split up, the more there is likely to be something fundamentally wrong with the relationship, which one of you is trying to tell the other.[3]

20. Score 1 for yes, 1 for more than anybody. You should love one another now, and if you don't, then you shouldn't be getting married! But just because you love each other now, doesn't mean things are guaranteed to work out.

1. Ibid   2. Ibid.   3. Ibid.

Results:

75 or less – there are issues here which need discussion.

75-90 – the odds are against you, but that doesn't mean that it won't work out.

90-105 – an unmarried couple of the average ages for first marriage (30 for men, 28 for women) would come here.

105-120 – this looks better.

121 or more – you have everything going for you, but there are no guarantees.

Of course, life isn't quite this predictable, and people with scores of 75 or less go on to have Golden Weddings ('and they told us it wouldn't last') whilst people who have scores of 121 or more go and get divorced.

Put back the going-away outfit – we only scored 56.

Resources

I Married You – Walter Trobisch, IVP, ISBN 0-85110-362-6.

The Mystery of Marriage – Mike Mason, Triangle SPCK, ISBN 0-28105051-1.

The Marriage Book – Nicky & Sila Lee – Alpha, ISBN 1-902750-27-6.

Your Wedding in the Church of England – Kevin Mayhew, ISBN 0-86209-802-5.

A Church Wedding – Ewen Gilchrist, Lion, ISBN 0-7459-4127-3.

Marriage Encounter/Engaged Encounter. The best place to look for information on this organisation is their website: http://www.marriageencounter.freeserve.co.uk. They provide weekends away for those who are married and those who are engaged, to give people the communication tools they need to help their married life, and to develop a vision for their future together. This is not a counselling weekend for those with problems, but an opportunity to deepen a relationship, whether it has been going for years, or is about to take the new step of marriage.

General Register Office for England and Wales, Smedley Hydro, Trafalgar Road, Southport PR8 2HH.
http://www.statistics.gov.uk/nsbase/registration/general_register.asp

Northern Ireland General Register Office, Oxford House, 49-55 Chichester Street, Belfast BT1 4HL.
http://www.nisra.gov.uk/gro

General Register Office for Scotland, Ladywell House, Ladywell Road, Edinburgh, EH12 7TF.
http://wood.ccta.gov.uk/grosweb/grosweb.nsf/pages/home

More Academic

Divorce and Second Marriage, Facing the Challenge – Kevin T. Kelly, Geoffrey Chapman, ISBN 0-225-66820-3.

Marriage, Divorce and the Church – Anthony E. Harvey, Darton, Longman & Todd, ISBN 0-232-52224-3.

Divorce in the New Testament – Raymond F. Collins, Michael Glazier Books, ISBN 0-8146-5691-9.

Marriage after Modernity – Adrian Thatcher, Sheffield Academic Press, ISBN 1-8507-5948-0.